The United States

Texas

Anne Welsbacher
ABDO & Daughters

visit us at
www.abdopub.com

Published by Abdo & Daughters, 4940 Viking Drive, Suite 622, Edina, Minnesota 55435.
Copyright © 1998 by Abdo Consulting Group, Inc., Pentagon Tower, P.O. Box 36036,
Minneapolis, Minnesota 55435 USA. International copyrights reserved in all countries.
No part of this book may be reproduced in any form without written permission from the
publisher.

Printed in the United States.

Cover and Interior Photo credits: Peter Arnold, Inc., Corbis-Bettmann

Edited by Lori Kinstad Pupeza
Contributing editor Brooke Henderson
Special thanks to our Checkerboard Kids—Annie O'Leary, Brandon Isakson, Laura Jones

All statistics taken from the 1990 census; The Rand McNally Discovery Atlas of The
United States.

Library of Congress Cataloging-in-Publication Data

Welsbacher, Anne, 1955-
    Texas / Anne Welsbacher.
    p. cm. -- (United States)
    Includes index.
    Summary: Describes the history, notable sights, people, recreations, and
    occupations of the Lone Star State.
    ISBN 1-56239-899-7
    1. Texas--Juvenile literature. [1. Texas.] I. title. II. Series: United States
    (series).
    F386.3.W45 1998
    976.4--dc21   97-38402
                                                     CIP
                                                     AC

Contents

Welcome to Texas

Texas is big! Of all the states, only Alaska is bigger. Once Texas was its very own country!

Texans work on the land—and in the sky! Texas has more farms and ranches than any other state. And a big space center in Texas runs all the space missions for the United States!

Cowboys once roamed the land of Texas. At one time, Texas had a flag with one star. So today Texas is called the Lone Star State.

Opposite page: Big Bend National Park in Texas.

Fast Facts

TEXAS
Capital
Austin (465,622 people)
Area
262,015 square miles
(678,616 sq km)
Population
17,059,805 people
Rank: 3rd
Statehood
December 29, 1845
(28th state admitted)
Principal rivers
Pecos River, Red River,
Rio Grande
Highest point
Guadalupe Peak;
8,749 feet (2,667 m)
Largest city
Houston (1,630,553 people)
Motto
Friendship
Song
"Texas, Our Texas"
Famous People
Stephen Austin, Sam Houston,
Lyndon B. Johnson, Willie
Nelson

*S*tate Flag

*B*luebonnet

*M*ockingbird

*P*ecan

About Texas

The Lone Star State

Detail area

TX
Texas's abbreviation

Borders: west (New Mexico, Mexico), north (Oklahoma), east (Arkansas, Louisiana), south (Gulf of Mexico, Mexico)

Nature's Treasures

Texas has more **petroleum** than almost any place in the world! Petroleum is a **mineral** used to make oil. Oil is used to run cars and many other machines.

The gas from Texas's land makes **electricity**—more than in any other state. Electricity runs radios, lights, and many other things. Texas soil also holds salt, sulfur, limestone, clay, iron, and even marble!

Texas land grows more cotton than any other state. Other Texas crops are hay and wheat. Texas grasses make good grazing for cattle. Texas Longhorns are a special kind of cattle found on Texas prairies.

Opposite page: Cattle grazing in a Texas pasture.

Texas

1500s to 1700s

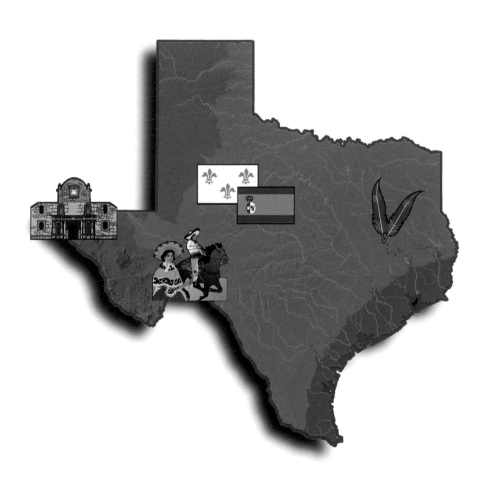

13

1821 to 1861

The Six-Flags State

 1821: Mexico breaks free from Spain and takes over the area. The flag of Mexico is the third to fly in Texas, after Spain and France.

 1836: Texas declares freedom from Mexico and flies its own flag over the Republic of Texas.

 1845: Texas becomes the 28th state. The U.S. flag is the fifth in Texas.

 1861: The Civil War begins. Texas **secedes** from the U.S. and joins the southern Confederate States of America, with a sixth flag.

Texas

1821 to 1861

1866 to 1993

Good Times, Hard Times

 1866: Cowboys drive herds of Texas cattle across the country.

 1901: A big oil field brings riches to many Texans.

 1980s: Oil prices fall and other energy sources are found. Texas seeks other ways to make money.

 1993: Texas mayor Henry Cisneros is given an important job in the United States government.

Texas

1866 to 1993

Texas's People

About 17 million people live in Texas. That is more than in any other state except California and New York.

Former presidents Dwight D. Eisenhower and Lyndon B. Johnson were born in Texas. Also born in Texas were the leaders Barbara Jordan, Ann Richards, and Henry Cisneros, who was the first Mexican-American to be the mayor of a big U.S. city.

Actor and comedian Steve Martin is from Waco, Texas. Joan Crawford, Mary Martin, and Larry Hagman also were born in Texas. Mary Martin starred in *Peter Pan*. Larry Hagman acted in a TV show about Texas called "Dallas."

Dancer Alvin Ailey was born in Rogers, Texas. He started a famous dance company. Writer Katherine Ann Porter was from Texas, too.

Blues singer Janis Joplin was from Port Arthur, Texas. Pianist Van Cliburn and rock-and-roll singer Buddy Holly were Texans, too.

Pianist Scott Joplin was from Texarkana, a town on the **border** between Texas and Arkansas. Scott Joplin first wrote a special music called ragtime.

Baseball pitcher Nolan Ryan was born in Texas. Other baseball greats from Texas were Frank Robinson, Ernie Banks, and Rogers Hornsby. Texan Willie Shoemaker won more horse races than any other jockey in his time.

Dwight D. Eisenhower

Nolan Ryan

Ann Richards

Texas's Cities

Many Texas cities are on the list of the 30 biggest cities in the United States!

The largest city in Texas is Houston. It is near Galveston Bay, which is next to a part of the ocean called the Gulf of Mexico. The Johnson Space Center is in Houston.

The next largest city is Dallas. It is in the north. Near Dallas is a big park with many rides called Six Flags Over Texas.

Next in size are San Antonio, El Paso, and Fort Worth. The sixth largest city is the capital, Austin.

Other cities are Corpus Christi, Lubbock, and Beaumont.

20

The skyline of Houston, Texas.

Texas's Land

Five other states could fit inside Texas and still have room left! All that land is divided into four different regions.

On the eastern side, near the Gulf of Mexico, is flat land called the Gulf Coastal Plain region. The Rio Grande River runs through the southern part of this area and ends up in the Gulf of Mexico.

The Rio Grande River is one of the longest in North America! It runs along the **border** of Texas and Mexico. Forests, hills, farmland, and lots of oil make up the rest of the land in the Gulf Coastal Plain region.

Starting at the top of Texas and running down the middle is

Central Lowland

Great Plains

Basin & Range Region

Gulf Coastal Plain

22

the Great Plains region. Most of this area is a dry, flat, treeless region.

The Central Lowland region covers the eastern edge of the Panhandle and the north-central part of the state. This area has lakes, rivers, prairies, and rolling plains.

In the western part of Texas is the Basin and Range region. This area has a series of rugged mountain ranges and dry, sandy, high plains. Here mountains and cliffs reach across the land.

Throughout Texas there are more than 500 kinds of grasses, and 4,000 kinds of wildflowers! Texas trees are oak, pine, sweet gum, cat's-claw, native pecan, and tupelo. Cactus plants also grow in the dry plains in the west.

Rio Grande River Canyon, Big Bend National Park.

Texans at Play

Texans love country and western music! Songs like "Home on the Range" were born in this cowboy state. Texans also love to play and listen to Mexican, folk, and rock-and-roll music.

Texans cheer for many football teams! The Dallas Cowboys have lots of fans in Texas. **College** teams are the Longhorns, the Aggies, and the Mustangs.

Texas has more fairs and festivals than any other state— more than 500 every year! The state fair is the biggest in the country. Many other events celebrate Mexican heritage, cowboys, pretty flowers, and much more.

Texas has its own special food. "Tex Mex" blends Mexican cooking and American cooking. Hot spices, barbecued beef, and special seafood dishes are other Texas favorites.

Horseback riding is a popular activity in Texas.

Texans at Work

Many Texans work in **manufacturing**. They make machines to pump oil out of the ground.

Texans also manufacture things to hold foods and drinks, like bottles and cans. They make parts for space crafts and other tools for the space center. Companies make computers in Texas.

Texans farm and work on ranches. Texas has more beef cattle than any other state. They also grow pecans, vegetables, and fruits, like peaches and watermelons.

Texans mine oil out of the ground. They also work in banks and in places **tourists** go, like motels and places to eat.

Opposite page: An oil drilling rig used to dig for oil.

Fun Facts

- The first world-wide airplane flight took off from Carswell Air Force Base in Fort Worth, Texas. The Lucky Lady II flew around the world in 1949.

- Most people who owned cattle herds put marks on their cattle. But one Texan did not. His name was Samuel Maverick. He was different from the others. Today, we call someone a "maverick" who is different from others in the "herd"!

- One of the world's largest nesting grounds of bats is at Bracken Cave in San Antonio, Texas. Sometimes as many as 20,000 bats fly out of the cave!

- The first live radio show of a football game was from a radio station in a **college** in Texas. The game was played in 1919.

•The Comal River in Texas is only 2 1/2 miles long!

•One in every three of the cowboys who rode the trails from 1866 to the 1880s were Mexican or African American.

The bats of Bracken Cave.

•In 1990, Elizabeth Watson became the first woman in the U.S. to be chief of police for a big city. She was named chief of police for Houston, Texas.

Glossary

Apaches: people who lived in Texas before people came from Spain; they fought many wars with other native people and with whites from Europe.

Border: the edge of something.

Caddo: people who lived in Texas before people came from Spain; they called themselves tejas, which means "friends."

College: a school you can go to after high school.

Electricity: a kind of power that runs TVs, fans, clocks, and many other things.

Era: a certain time in history.

Juneteenth: a celebration every June 19, the day in 1865 that Texas slaves were finally freed, two months after President Lincoln had freed all southern state slaves.

Manufacture: to make things.

Mastodon: a big animal like a buffalo that lived thousands of years ago.

Mineral: something found in the ground like coal, diamonds, or oil.

Petroleum: a mineral used to make oil.

Secede: to break away.

Tonkawas: people who lived in Texas before people came from Spain.

Tourist: a person who travels places for fun.

Internet Sites

Texas Best
http://www.texas-best.com/
This has everything about Texas. Its music, people, sports, festivals, animals, arts, and much more.

Texas Trails
http://www.lone-star.net/mall/main-areas/txtrails.htm
Texas is a unique dominion that draws its present-day identity from six different countries as well as from the ancient that preceded even the first explorers. Mexican and Native American traditions figure prominently in the state alongside the cultures of the Central and Eastern European settlers who arrived much later. A great historical journey.

These sites are subject to change. Go to your favorite search engine and type in Texas for more sites.

PASS IT ON

Tell Others Something Special About Your State

To educate readers around the country, pass on interesting tips, places to see, history, and little unknown facts about the state you live in. We want to hear from you!

To get posted on ABDO & Daughters website, e-mail us at "mystate@abdopub.com"

Index